CW00970516

Writing Reports that Get Results

Using Language's Power to Persuade

Ian Douglas

Acknowledgement

I am indebted to Barclay Simpson for sponsoring the publication of this book. Barclay Simpson (www.barclaysimpson.com), is a leading global corporate governance recruitment and executive search consultancy, with offices in London, New York, Dubai. Hong Kong and Singapore. Opinions expressed in the book are those of the author, and do not necessarily represent those of Barclay Simpson.

Table of Contents

Preface

Internal audit, risk management, compliance and health and safety reports can be particularly difficult to write. You often have to bring unpalatable truths to the attention of management. The main aim of the report should be to achieve corrective action. Corrective action is easier to achieve if you can get management on your side, rather than becoming defensive and self-justifying.

I spent about 35 years in internal audit and risk management roles, and for 25 years was a senior manager or head of department. In that time I estimate I wrote or edited well over 4000 reports. These covered the whole range of audit and risk management areas, from straightforward reports of branch audits, risk reviews, technically complex computer audit reports, to Audit Committee and Board reports.

This book describes some of the lessons I learned through practical experience over a long time. It includes how to write concisely and simply, and how to make complex issues easier to read and understand. But equally important is using the power of language to persuade, rather than antagonise the reader.

Report writing isn't mathematics; there is no one right answer. English continues to evolve, and what jars with one person may seem correct modern usage to another. Don't become negative if you disagree with any aspects of the text. Give it due consideration, and if you still disagree just ignore it and move to the next point.

At the start of my business life, report-writing tools were non-existent. Reports were typed on manual typewriters by a typing pool, and making even minor changes could require significant retyping. Now staff type reports themselves, and increasingly they will dictate, not to a typing pool but directly into speech recognition software. Altering or introducing text is now easy. Reports can be reviewed on-line, commented on, and changes proposed or introduced by managers in another continent on the same day.

Microsoft Word can also flag up problems in grammar and style. This can be helpful, albeit not all of Word's suggestions will be appropriate, and correct text can often be flagged by Word as an error. The book also explores how these tools can be used to best effect. No doubt they will get better in future generations of word-processing software.

This book is deliberately short – it should be possible to read it and complete the two examples in under three hours. Inexperienced report writers should gain a great deal from it, and I believe even experienced report writers will gain something. To reinforce change, diarise to re-visit the text once a month for three months. Inexperienced writers should read the whole text again; experienced writers should highlight any useful points, and on re-reading will only need a few minutes to review the items they have highlighted.

Strangely enough (as far as some of my colleagues were concerned), I enjoyed editing reports, and passing my love of concise and simple English onto my staff. Producing a well-written report that achieves results can leave you with a feeling of pride and satisfaction.

If you find the book useful, I would be very grateful if you would review it on the retailer's website. I am an independent author and so, unlike a major publisher, I don't have a marketing department. Therefore I depend on satisfied readers to help publicise the book.

Ian Douglas
Hampshire
U.K.

1. Introduction

On 9 August 1940, after the fall of France, and when Britain was fighting for its survival, Winston Churchill sent a memo to his War Cabinet titled "Brevity". This began:

"To do our work, we all have to read a mass of papers. Nearly all of them are far too long. This wastes time, while energy has to be spent on looking for the essential points."

A report is the shop window of any department whose role is to review and make recommendations. It doesn't matter how hard you work, if you don't report in a simple, straightforward, easy to read way, your recommendations are less likely to be implemented and your effort will be wasted.

Technical staff may be highly qualified in their area of specialisation, but they do not necessarily have report writing skills. Also, inexperienced staff often can't understand the importance of good report writing – they don't understand the need to sell their work and findings to a busy and sometimes sceptical management, who may look at issues from a different perspective. Staff often need help and training to produce succinct, well laid out reports that hit the mark.

The report is what management acts on, if they understand and agree with the conclusions and recommendations. The report is the part of your work that they see, and therefore what they judge you by. External consultancies understand this and put a great deal of effort into presenting well-written reports. Some of the larger consultancies have departments whose role is to edit and format reports to a high standard, reports that their technical staff have drafted.

External consultancies are also very aggressive in trying to sell their services. If external providers can persuade management that they can produce a better product than internal functions, management often decide to outsource activities to these consultancies. So internal functions must be able to present their reports to at least the same standard as a large external consultancy.

This text provides guidance on producing clear, concise and easy to read reports. It covers the basics of structuring a report. However, as many departments have developed their own formats and are happy with them, the focus of this guidance is on using the power of language to make any report easier to read and understand, irrespective of the report structure.

Chapters 2 to 8 of the guide cover the following:

2. **Report basics and structure:** It is vital for clarity and readability to have a simple and easy to follow structure.

3. **Language and tone:** Is the tone suitable for delivering the message? Report writers should be sensitive to the culture of the organisation they are working in. I have written this guide in a colloquial style, as recommended by Winston Churchill (see Chapter 4). This might not be acceptable in some organisations. The style of the organisation should be used in preparing the report.

4. **Writing concisely and simply:** Is the English used simple and to the point? Concise and simple writing can make a major difference to the readability of the document, and is what busy executives expect from professionals.

5. **Illustrating reports:** Charts and diagrams can be an excellent way of presenting complex numeric and financial data. Photographs can also communicate evidence very effectively in some cases.

6. **Editing and typographical checking:** This is essential to provide a polished, professional product.

7. **Tools to help in report writing:** Setting up your word processing package properly, and using the facilities it provides fully, can be a shortcut to producing a professional report.

8. **Other issues:** The versions of English to be used, using PowerPoint to produce reports, grading reports, and improving report writing in a department are explored.

As should be standard for any good report, detail is relegated to the appendices:

Appendix 1 gives examples of badly expressed words and phrases, and their alternatives.

Appendix 2 shows ten English words that are easily confused.

Appendix 3 provides suggested answers for the two exercises in the text.

2. Report Basics and Structure

Identifying the Audience

The first major step is to identify who the readers are, and therefore who you are you writing for. Is it:

- The Board or Board committee, such as the Audit, Risk or Compliance Committee?
- Senior executive management?
- Line management who understand the detail?

The reality is that you are often writing for all of the above.

Also, consider whether the report could be read by external bodies such as regulators, who may lack the perspective internal readers can bring to issues raised in the report.

One of the challenges for any report writer is that you may have three or four distinct audiences, each with different levels of knowledge and objectives in reading the report. However, if you can get the report structure, writing style and tone correct, it is possible to meet the needs of these different audiences.

A Basic Report Structure

Most reports have an executive summary, a detailed section, and often appendices.

The **executive summary** should be written in as non-technical language as possible, summarising the main issues in a way that can be understood by a layman. The executive summary should be concise, easy to read, with issues cross-referred to the relevant area in the detailed section for those who want more information.

The **detailed section** usually includes findings, recommendation or agreed action, manager responsible for implementation, and action date. As this section goes into detail, language that is more technical may be used if necessary, but this should be kept to a minimum.

> *"If a report relies on detailed analysis of some complicated factors, or on statistics, these should be set out in an Appendix."*
> Winston Churchill's "Brevity" memo, 9 August 1940.

The real detail should be relegated to **appendices**, for readers to refer to if they wish. They are for reference when necessary, rather than reading in full.

The assignment working papers are usually used as the basis of large parts of the report's detailed findings section and appendices. This information can be either manually "cut and paste" into the report, or automatically transferred if an electronic workings papers system is used. Therefore clear and simple English, as described in chapter 4, should be used in the working papers. This has the double benefit of making the working papers easier to understand, and reducing editing at the report writing stage.

The report, and sections within the report, should adopt the following basic principles.

Use Meaningful Headings

Headings help give a report structure, and should be clear and specific. This orientates the reader, prepares the reader for the content of the section, and helps the reader to navigate through the report.

Start at the End

Reports are not detective stories. Busy senior managers should be provided with the conclusions first (the executive summary), and then the evidence that supports the conclusions (the detailed findings).

This principle also applies to individual findings. The reader should not have to read paragraph after paragraph of evidence before being informed of the point that the evidence leads up to. The answer, that is the conclusion, should be given first. Then the more detailed background and evidence can be laid out. It is much easier to read and understand a detailed point if the fundamental issue is summarised in one sentence before the detailed evidence is provided.

If senior management feel they understand and agree with the point after reading the first sentence or two, they may decide to skip the more detailed evidence and move onto the next point in the report. This is their prerogative - their time is usually extremely limited.

Start Each Section with the Major Issues

The first issues raised or findings in the report should tie the reader in. Successful popular authors know this. Make your strongest point, or most significant finding, first in each section. Don't lead with minor issues.

Report Presentation

Attractive and simple layout can make reports easier to read. Layout can be slapdash in this age when reports are generally typed by the author, rather than a professional typist or secretary. Any department that regularly issues reports should devise a report template for an attractive and easy-to-read report. Having a template to work with can also help to speed up report production.

3. Language and Tone

Adapting Your Language to Your Audience

We have already stressed that the audience for the report will shape the writing style you should use. For example, in this text I have chosen to use contractions such as *it's* for *it is*, and *haven't* for *have not*. Using a writing style that is close to a speaking style makes documents easier to read than using a formal style. However if I was writing a report for a very tradition organisation I would adopt a more formal writing style.

This also affects some aspect of grammar. For example, traditionalist will not start sentences or paragraphs with *and* or *but*. I have never really understood why this was considered wrong. After all, this was good enough for the Bible – "And God said "let there be light". The only explanation that may hold some truth is that young children often speak in very short sentences starting with *and* or *but*. For example:

"I saw a cat. And a black kitten. But the cat didn't want to play."

So this was an attempt to encourage children to use more complex sentence structures! In any case *and* or *but* are now widely used to start sentences and paragraphs in major establishment publications such as The Economist or The Wall Street Journal. In fact if you split lengthy sentences into smaller sentences, you are likely to start many of the shorter sentences with *and* or *but*.

But if you think your audience might find starting sentences or paragraphs with *and* or *but* annoying, or consider it demonstrates a lack of education, I recommend you adopt a more traditional style.

Adopting a Style to Influence, Not Antagonise

Inexperienced staff often believe that they have to justify their existence by identifying major issues. Therefore they may present their findings in an overly critical and sensational way. This usually isn't a constructive approach, as it can generate a defensive response. A report writer must be conscious of how readers will interpret the report.

Management often work very hard, and yet there may be significant issues needing attention in their area. A very critical report can affect the career of the manager whose area is being criticised, and in some cases can lead to the manager's dismissal. Management can interpret report wording, used by the report's author without thinking, as adversarial, unfair and hurtful. If this is the case it will generate a defensive and negative response. It is better to use what I call a balanced/constructive reporting style, and only adopt a strongly critical style where there is evidence of negligence or incompetence.

Facts can be coloured by the way they are expressed – politicians and public relations executives know this!

Consider the following statement:

A review of customers' complaints revealed that 28.9% of complaints were from customers annoyed by the heavy-handed and bureaucratic requirements for evidence of purchase before a refund was made.

This could also be presented as follows:

A review of customer complaints revealed that 28.9% of complaints were from customers experiencing difficulties in complying with the department's requirements for evidence of purchase before a refund was made.

The facts are the same, but the tone makes a difference to the message. An unintentional but heavy-handed choice of words is likely to result in a defensive response from the manager whose area is being reviewed, and so they may be less open to making changes.

Of course, there are occasions when it is appropriate to issue a highly critical report, but if you do use highly critical wording be sure that this is the message you wish to communicate. Consider if you are unintentionally being overcritical by your choice of wording.

The following table gives some examples of wording which can have a similar underlying meaning, but a very different tone. The first column is very critical, the second column less so. In many circumstances a finding could be expressed using either option.

CRITICAL	BALANCED/CONSTRUCTIVE
the review uncovered that xx	the review identified that xx
the system has serious inadequacies	if the system were revised, it would be possible to....
no attention has been given to xx	xx should be addressed
failed to accomplish	could be accomplished by
unacceptable	control would be improved by
inadequate controls	control would be improved by
extravagant expenditure	expenditure outside corporate policy

If your objective is to achieve beneficial change, a balanced/constructive approach to expressing findings and recommendations can often be the most productive. Using a balanced/constructive style isn't letting management "off the hook" if it is supported by a robust approach to following up agreed recommendations to confirm that they have been implemented. However, it is important not to draw back from being critical where criticism is justified. Just ensure that you are being critical when it is warranted, and not by making a poor choice of language.

Adopting Gender Neutral Language

English has its limitations. The singular third personal pronoun is either male or female. At one time it was common to use the male pronoun when referring to roles except where that role was clearly female. This is no longer appropriate, and should never have been appropriate. Some readers will be offended by the presumption that senior roles are automatically held by men.

One alternative is to use "he or she", rather than simply "he". However, this is a cumbersome approach that readers usual find irritating, particularly if used frequently.

A number of strategies are available to avoid using the clumsy "he or she" option. One approach that works in some circumstances is simply to delete the personal pronoun from the sentence. For example:

Bad: The manager should review his subordinates' training needs every six months.

Better: The manager should review subordinates' training needs every six months.

Another approach that can be used is to pluralise the text, for example to refer to managers rather than manager. That allows gender independent pronouns such as they, their, and them to be used instead of he, his, him.

Using this approach on the above example:

Better: Managers should review their subordinates' training needs every six months.

Or if there is only one manager, consider using *each,* rather than the personal pronoun:

Better: The manager should review each subordinate's training needs every six months.

Another approach is to reword the sentence rather than use the personal pronoun:

Better: The manager should review the training needs of subordinates every six months.

As shown above there are a number of options. Some read better than others, depending on the specifics of the example. Use what is most appropriate and reads well.

4. Writing Concisely and Simply

Let us have an end to phrases such as these: "It is also of importance to bear in mind the following considerations........", or "Consideration should be given to the possibility of carrying into effect ...." Most of these woolly phrases are mere padding, which can be left out altogether, or replaced by a single word. Let us not shrink from using the short expressive phrase, even if it is conversational.
Winston Churchill's "Brevity" memo to the War Cabinet, 9 August 1940.

Inexperienced writers sometimes think that writing in a pompous, wordy style demonstrates their level of accomplishment and education, and impresses the reader. (Note that I have used the plural in the previous sentence, to avoid using the singular personal pronoun!) In fact, writing in a pompous, wordy style shows the opposite. Clear, simple writing can make a major difference to readability. Senior executives have a massive reading load, and therefore greatly appreciate clear, concise and well-written material.

But what are the basic principles of clear and simple writing?

Use Short Sentences

Most sentences should be short and simple – short, punchy sentences have more impact than long, rambling ones. An average sentence lengths of 15 to 17 words is ideal, and certainly keep the average length below 20 words. Sentences should usually only convey one idea. However, a report that consists entirely of short sentences is the writing equivalent of machine gun fire rather than music, and irritates after a while. A few long sentences add variety and actually improve readability.

Long sentences that make several points can be broken down into shorter sentences. If these all have a common theme, each point can be presented as a short, concise bullet point, or as part of a numbered list of issues.

Bullet Points

The following example shows how bullet points can make dense text easier to understand.

We checked 25 credit notes, and we identified 8 cases where there was no evidence to support the credit, 6 credit notes of over £1000 which were authorised by clerical staff rather than supervisors, indicating that appropriate authorisation controls are not present in the computer system, 7 cases where there was no evidence of the goods having been returned, and in 6 cases VAT charged on the original sale had not been appropriately accounted for in the credit note.

A real mouthful, particularly as it would be in the middle of a lengthy report. It is far easier to understand when presented as follows:

We checked 25 credit notes, and noted:

- 8 cases without documentary evidence to support the credit.
- 6 credit notes of over £1000 authorised by clerical staff rather than supervisors. This also indicates that appropriate authorisation controls are not present in the computer system.
- 7 cases without evidence of the goods having been returned.
- 6 cases where VAT charged on the original sale had not been accounted for in the credit note.

Avoid Jargon and Specialist Language

Jargon should always be avoided, and ideally specialist language such as technical terms, abbreviations and acronyms should only be used if all readers of the report are likely to understand the terms. Wherever possible use everyday words that convey meaning clearly and directly. In exceptional circumstances you may have no option but to use technical terms. If so, provide a glossary. It is good practice to provide a glossary even if you believe that all readers are likely to understand the specialist language used. Often not all readers do understand, and those who do can ignore the glossary as it is at the end of the report.

Use Clear and Concise English

Tightly written text is quicker to read and, more importantly, easier to understand than wordy text. "Dead wood" words and phrases get in the reader's way and obscure the meaning.

There are three main types of verbose text:

- Unnecessarily complex and longwinded language.
- Redundant words, including intensifiers.
- Using nouns constructed from verbs, rather than the verbs themselves.

We shall consider each category, and give a few examples. There are more examples in the appendix. However, even the appendix only illustrates the problem. English is an almost infinitely flexible language, so a writer can make up many more examples of verbose wording!

Complex and Longwinded Language

The following phrases just bulk out the text, delaying the message. There are many other examples in the appendix.

Complex	Simple
despite the fact that	although
due to the fact that	because
during which time	while
at the present time	now

Eliminating Redundant Words and Intensifiers

Another example of verbiage is the use of redundant words and intensifiers.

Bad	Good
advanced planning	planning
a difficult task	difficult
difficult challenge	challenge
end result	result
past experience	experience
very	(consider omitting)

There are many other examples in the appendix. Sometimes intensifiers are useful in adding emphasise, but in most cases this isn't necessary. Often they just bulk out the text and so reduce clarity.

Using a Noun Phrase Rather than a Verb

This is called nominalisation in grammar speak. Less frequently than verbs, adjectives or adverbs can be used to create the noun phrase. Examples on nominalisation are:

Nominalisation	Verb Form
the avoidance of	avoid
start an investigation	investigate
have a meeting	meet

The appendix contains further examples.

Nominalisations are formal and less direct than simple verbs. Some nominalisations are appropriate. However, widespread use of nominalisation in a report increases wordiness and formality, sometimes to the point of pomposity, and makes text more difficult to follow.

Using the Active rather than Passive Voice

In the active voice the subject of the sentence acts upon something. In the passive voice, the subject is acted upon. For example:

The project management team introduced the change. (Active)

The change was introduced by the project management team. (Passive)

Active voice is shorter, more direct and introduces clear accountability, and therefore usually the best approach. But if you are following the balanced/constructive approach referred to earlier, there are occasions when you may want to use the passive tense, to make critical remarks less direct.

Almost all documents contain some passive voice text; it is when there is a great deal of passive voice text that reports become verbose. So as part of report editing consider if any passive sentences could be better expressed in the active voice.

Commas Can Make a Difference

Badly placed commas usually make text more difficult to read, rather than changing the meaning. However, there are occasions when repositioning or adding commas can change the meaning of text significantly, as can be seen in the following:

Woman without her man is nothing.

Which of the following correctly represents the intended meaning?

Woman without her man, is nothing.

Woman, without her, man is nothing.

I don't know what the writer intended!

Case Study

Let us bring many if the points in chapters 2 to 4 together in the following example. In the real world editing would be done in one step, but in order to understand the process better I suggest the case study is undertaken in two stages:

a) Identify unnecessarily wordy text, as described in chapter 4.
b) Apply the other report writing principles identified in chapters 2 and 3.

Suggested answers are in Appendices 3a and 3b.

Weaknesses in Locally Developed Complaints Management System.

Significance: Very High

Complaints statistics are prepared for the Customer Services Review Committee and the Board by manually inputting data from the complaints management system into an Excel spreadsheet. The development of this spreadsheet took place in the Customer Services department, and it is used to perform an analysis of complaints data on a weekly basis in various ways in order to show trends and changes, and produces a presentation of the output using a series of charts. Although the complaints management system provides the raw data, this system does not have sophisticated analysis and visual presentation tools.

The spreadsheet was prepared by Mr A Smith, a Complaints Handling Officer, and a computer enthusiast without a formal I.T. background. The end result of this is a spreadsheet with major weaknesses as outlined below.

With regards to the spreadsheet logic, this has not been subject to a review and there is not a formal testing process in place when developing the formula. The system is still being enhanced and changes are made regularly. However, in view of the fact that there is no version control system in place, there is a risk that a wrong version of a spreadsheet could be used. We are also concerned that neither the code nor the data is backed up, or subject to the organisation's contingency arrangements. Another weakness is that the spreadsheet logic is undocumented, making maintenance by anyone other than Mr Smith a very difficult task.

Data is input manually from the complaints handling system, without a formal checking process. Therefore, there is a risk in relation to input errors being undetected.

Because of this, we consider this is a very high significance issue as errors could result in complaints trends going undetected. This would delay corrective action, and the end result would be poor customer service. In addition, this could also result in regulatory breaches.

Recommendations
Because of the above weaknesses it is our recommendation that the spreadsheet be placed under the control of the I.T. department, which should carry out a review of the logic, and then after this review has taken place, place the system under the usual controls for a production system. Furthermore, the Customer Services Department should introduce a checking process for data manually input to the system, to identify any data input errors. (Significance Very High).

5. Illustrating Reports

Using Charts

The old saying "a picture is worth a thousand words" is true, and should be extended to charts and diagrams as well. Charts and diagrams can be an excellent way to present complex financial and numerical data. It is easier to interpret data, spot trends and make comparisons, when the data is shown pictorially than when it is simply described in words. Charts and diagrams improve readability and increase impact.

However it is important to still state the message or conclusion, rather than leave the reader to interpret the data. The graphic should support the message, not replace it.

Using colours can lift the chart, but be aware that some readers may print the report on a black and white printer. If this could happen, hatchings and shading as well as colour should be used so that the chart is easily understood in black and white.

It is not necessary to use Excel to prepare a chart, although this is an option. Modern versions of Microsoft Word have sophisticated chart-making facilities. This is in the **INSERT** tab, where the **illustrations** group has a chart feature.

The three most commonly used types of charts are pie charts, line charts and bar charts.

Pie Charts

Pie charts can be used to compare quantities, either as numbers or as percentages of a whole. A pie chart can work well when there are up to seven or eight components, but beyond that it becomes difficult for the reader to interpret the data.

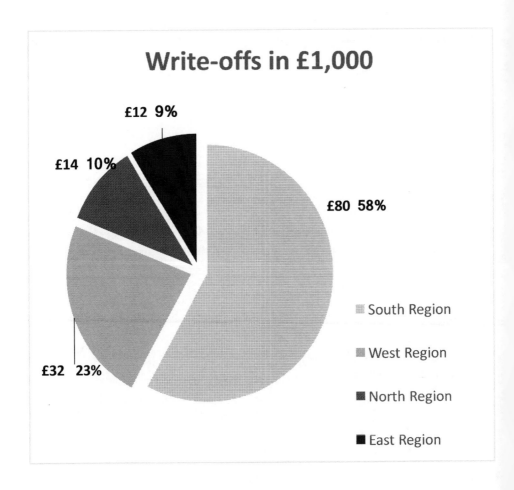

Bar Charts

Bar charts are another widely used method of presenting data. Bar charts are useful for comparing quantities between areas, and showing how they change over time, as in the example below.

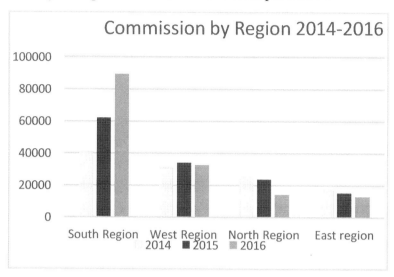

Line Charts

Line charts connect individual numeric values, and are a useful way of displaying trends over time, for example:

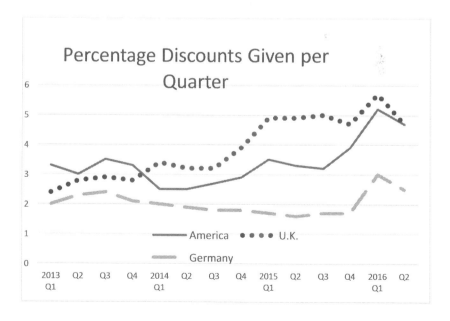

There are many other diagram types available, such as the scatter gram and area chart.

Photographs

Most mobile phones now have a camera, and most staff are experienced in using them. Photographs can add impact and provide tangible evidence that is difficult to refute. For example, a photograph of a disorganized warehouse, a security fence with gaps, or a computer room with disordered and unsafe electric cabling.

If a scanner isn't readily available, another use of photographs is to copy documents for inclusion in the working papers and in reports where appropriate.

Other Opportunities for Illustrating Reports

Two other Word features can be used to enhance reports:

- Word's SmartArt facility is useful for adding diagrams, such as organization charts, to reports.
- The screenshot feature allows screenshots of any window that is open on your desktop to be included in a document.

Both these features are available in the *illustrations* group in the **INSERT** tab in recent versions of MS Word.

6. Editing and Typographical Checking

Editing

In this chapter we focus on editing the report for structure, writing style and clarity, and then carrying out a detailed proofreading review for typographical errors.

In many departments, such as internal audit departments, the report author will carry out an editing and proofreading review, and then forward the report and the assignment working papers to the team manager. The manager then carries out an independent review of the assignment working papers and the report, to confirm the quality of the work and that all points identified have been covered appropriately in the report. This very involved topic is covered in auditing textbooks, and is out of scope of this guide. This guide concentrates on the report author's and manager's review of the report for structure, writing style and clarity, and then proofreading the report for typographical errors.

If you have just finished drafting a report, it is important to have a break between finishing the draft and editing it. Ideally leave the report overnight, and start the edit when you can look at it with fresh eyes in the morning. But if you are working to a very tight timetable and this is not possible, please at least have a long coffee break before tackling the editing process. It is very important to come at this task with a fresh perspective, so do have a break between writing and editing.

After I have drafted a report, and before I start editing it, I carry out a spelling and grammar check using Word's inbuilt spelling and grammar checking functions. I repeat this later, when proofreading for typographical errors. Some people argue that there is little point in spelling or grammar checking before editing, as you are likely to make structural and textual during editing. However the spelling and grammar check can be carried out quickly. I find that it is much easier to concentrate on style and clarity if the spelling and the worst grammar mistakes have been corrected in the text I am reviewing.

I use Microsoft Word, and I find the spell checker very helpful, but the grammar checker less so. Because of this, and as the text format may change during editing, I often ignore all but the worst grammatical "errors" until I am happy with the report structure, writing style and clarity. Be wary of accepting recommended changes without thought when tired, as they may be inappropriate and you can introduce errors.

For some reason known only to Microsoft, Word requires you to carry out a spell and grammar check before it compiles the readability statistics that show average sentence length and indicate reading complexity. Even though you are at an early stage in the review process, it is worthwhile looking at these figures, to see if the report has a serious problem in these areas. See chapter 7 for more details about readability statistics.

Reviewing for Structure, Writing Style and Clarity

Earlier in this guide we covered the main elements of clear and simple writing. In summary, the questions that should be asked are:

- Is the report well laid out, with consistent spacing?
- Is it easy to navigate through by the use of sensible headings?
- Is the tone appropriate?
- Does each section start with a clear summary of the point? (Start at the end).
- Is gender neutral language used?
- Is the English used simple and concise? Does the report contain any longwinded expressions that can be simplified, or redundant words that can be removed?
- Are there any sentences in the passive voice that would read better if the active voice was used?
- Are there any noun phrases that could be reworded as verbs?
- Are there a variety of sentence lengths, with an average sentence length less than 20 words?
- Are jargon, technical terms and abbreviations avoided

- wherever possible, and if used are they explained in a glossary?
- In summary, can the report be understood easily?

Once the above checks have been completed, and changes made, it is time to carry out the last report review phase, proofreading for typographical errors.

Proofreading for Typographical Errors

Proofreading for typographical errors, (often abbreviated to typos), is the detailed checking of a report to identify:

- Spelling errors.
- Grammatical errors.
- Formatting errors.
- Textual errors, such as missing or repeating words.

The best way to start is to run your word processing package's spelling and grammar checker again. The spelling, grammar and style checkers in word processors are very useful, and should be used on all reports. But as the following poem shows, the technology has limitations:

> I have a little spell checker,
> It came with my PC,
> It plainly marks for my revue,
> Miss takes I cannot sea.
> I've run this poem threw it,
> I'm sure you're pleased too no,
> Its letter perfect in its weigh,
> My checker told me sews!

Word 2013's spell checker did not detect any errors in the above text. A spell checker will not detect an error that results in a word in the spell checker's dictionary. So, although it is very useful, don't think that this will detect all spelling errors.

Grammar and style checking is even more difficult for a computer software package. Grammar and style checkers are useful, but as English is such a complex language they are only partly effective in identifying issues, and often wrongly flag well-written text as containing errors. Word takes a very traditional approach to grammar and style, although as described in chapter 7 this can be customised a little, as can Word's spell checker. Word's suggestions should be considered just that, as suggestions. Only make changes if you agree with them.

After running the spelling, grammar and style checkers, it is time to carry out a detailed manual check.

It can be very difficult to see minor typographical errors in a report you have written. The brain wants to read quickly and concentrate on the meaning of the text. You also tend to read what you think you have written, and have to force yourself to slow down and concentrate on the text. Some people recommend reading aloud, but this might not go down well in a busy office! Another more practical approach is to read with a sheet of paper under each line as you scan the text. This helps you to concentrate on the line of text you are reading.

As part of the editing process, a reviewer who has not been involved in writing the report should carry out the review. In a well-organised department, before being issued reports will always be read by a manager who has not carried out the review. This is a very useful way to get a fresh perspective, which may detect issues not identified by the report writer, who is too close to the text and often blind to errors. To save wasting paper I carry out my initial checking on the screen, but always carry out my final checking on a paper version of the report. I don't know if this is an age thing, but I can often find issues on the paper version I miss on the screen.

If you are in a department without a predefined review process for reports, try to get an independent person to review the report. If this isn't possible (perhaps the report is highly confidential), it is even more important that you put the draft to one side for some time, so that you can come back to it fresh. Then review it carefully several times. This can be tedious, but it is essential if you want to produce a quality product.

Proofreading Exercise

There are a number of mistakes in this paragraph. Some of them would not be detected buy an automated spell and crammer chick. How many thongs can you find wrong. It is no easy, particularly if you have too reed a long, badly structured piper, with many moor tissues.

The above text has been checked for spelling, grammar and style by Word 2013. I accepted all of Word's recommendations. How many mistakes can you find? See appendix 3c for the answer.

7. Tools to Help in Report Writing

Microsoft Word has a range of tools to support good writing, and to assist in checking text. I don't believe these are used widely enough as they are often not fully understood. This chapter summarises the most useful Word features for proofing reports, and how these can be customised. It assumes that you have a basic understanding of Word. However Word's features change. This text provides an overview of Word for Windows 2013, which is widely used. Other versions, particularly pre-2007 versions, may differ in the features available, and how they are implemented.

Word 2016 as available in 2016 has more rudimentary grammar checking than previous versions, and no style checking options. Microsoft is trying to improve their grammar and style checking in Word 2016, but not finding it easy, because of the complexities of English. Word's grammar and style checking rules are being rewritten, and details are not yet available of these changes. Hopefully when Microsoft release an update to Word 2016, grammar and style checking will be much improved over earlier versions of Word.

This chapter only provides an overview of what is available in Word 2013. It is best to refer to a detailed Word manual, to check what features are available with your version, and for detailed guidance on how to use them. Introductory Word manuals often don't cover some of these features, or only cover them at a superficial level.

Customising Spelling and Grammar Checking Settings

Language Setting

We discussed using Microsoft Word's spelling and grammar checker in chapter 6. Ensure that this is set up for the language version you are writing in. You can do this by going to the **REVIEW** tab, clicking on the **Language** button, and then selecting the **Set Proofing Language** option. This brings up the above box, from which you can make your choice. For English, many versions of Word offer a choice of U.K., U.S., Canadian and Australian.

Do not check the "Detect language automatically" option, as in practice this doesn't always work.

Modifying Spelling and Grammar Checking Options

You can select a range of spelling and grammar options by going to the **FILE** tab in Word, clicking on the **Options** button, and then on the **proofing** option. This brings up the following screen, from which you can make your choice.

ABC✓ Change how Word corrects and formats your text.

AutoCorrect options

Change how Word corrects and formats text as you type: [AutoCorrect Options...]

When correcting spelling in Microsoft Office programs

☑ Ignore words in UPPERCASE
☑ Ignore words that contain numbers
☑ Ignore Internet and file addresses
☑ Flag repeated words
☐ Enforce accented uppercase in French
☐ Suggest from main dictionary only
[Custom Dictionaries...]

French modes: [Traditional and new spellings ▾]
Spanish modes: [Tuteo verb forms only   ▾]

When correcting spelling and grammar in Word

☑ Check spelling as you type
☑ Mark grammar errors as you type
☑ Frequently confused words
☑ Check grammar with spelling
☑ Show readability statistics

Writing Style: [Grammar & Style ▾]   [Settings...]
[Check Document]

Exceptions for: [📄 Document5   ▾]
☐ Hide spelling errors in this document only

Autocorrect Options, and Settings

Clicking on either of two boxes shown in the screenshot on page 33, **Autocorrect Options,** and **Settings,** gives a range of further options.

Autocorrect Options

Autocorrect Options as shown below provide a number of checks that can be switched on or off. The "replace text as you type" table contains hundreds of items, and additional items can be added by the user.

Settings Options

Click the **Settings** box shown on page 33 and a number of detailed grammar and style checking options appear, a small section of which are shown below.

Using the options available, it is possible to fine-tune spelling, grammar and style checking significantly so that it is more closely in line with the writing style of the department. As you can see, I have deleted the tick in the Contractions check box, since I decided to use contractions ("I've" for "I have", for example), in this text. I also cleared the tick from another style option lower in the selection and therefore not shown in the table. "Sentences beginning with And, But and Hopefully" can be flagged as an error or ignored, depending on the choice made.

But grammar and style checking is rather basic and subject to errors. Only treat any issues raised by this function as justifying consideration; don't automatically accept them. Hopefully Microsoft will improve this in future versions of Word.

Add-ins

It isn't widely known that it is possible to add apps to Word 2013 to provide increased functionality. This is available on the **INSERT** tab, in the **Add-ins** group. This allows you to change the dictionary that Word uses, for example. The app that I use on long documents is the Consistency Checker. This has some additional features over most spelling and grammar checkers, including identifying inconsistencies in:

- use of hyphens,
- numbering e.g. using numerics or spelling out numbers,
- use of abbreviations (e.g. NASA and Nasa).

Commenting on Text

A reviewer can add comments to a document, using the **Comments** group in the **REVIEW** tab. It is best to review the document in print layout view, as some people have noted on the web that using this feature in other views can produce erratic results. Reviewers should select the text that they want to comment on, and then click the **New Comments** button.

You may want to add a comment to remind you to check something later, for example. The comments feature is particularly useful when a document is being reviewed by a number of people. Word records the comments in a revisions pane, and the name of the person making the comment is recorded with the comment. The name is taken from the computer, so if a reviewer is using someone else's computer, the computer owner's initials will be recorded in the pane.

The comments facility is useful when a reviewer is reviewing a document on the screen. It is a particularly helpful feature if the reviewer is in a different location from the report author, as it enables what is in effect a dialogue about the report.

Track Changes Facility

This is another excellent facility for reviewing documents. Instead of adding comments, the reviewer can propose revisions to the document without the original text being lost. Proposed revisions are indicated by a vertical line in the left margin. In the document, insertions are underlined and deletions are crossed out. As you hover your cursor over the proposed change, the name of the person proposing it, and the time, are displayed.

The track changes feature can be switched on or off in the **tracking** group in the **REVIEW** tab. The document can be displayed with or without the changes. Changes can be accepted or rejected by the document owner.

Controlling Changes

If a number of people are reading or working on a document, it is important that the editing process isn't a free for all. The document owner may want to allow some people to simply read the document, others to leave comments, and others to propose changes using the track changes feature, so they can be reviewed and checked before being accepted. Word 2013 allows this. In the **FILE** tab there is a **protect document** button, which gives access to a range of options to restrict editing of the document.

Removing Any Embarrassing Data

I have experience of reports being issued electronically without changes that were proposed by reviewers having been accepted. These might not be immediately obvious to the report author, depending on what options are current in the drop-down box in the **tracking** group in the **REVIEW** tab. But if the reader goes to the **REVIEW** tab, and in the **tracking** group chooses **all mark-up** in the drop-down box, these become visible. Likewise comments can be left in the report.

This allows the report recipient to trace through the edits and in effect read the early draft of the report not intended for distribution. This could be embarrassing, for example if insensitive comments are made or a finding or opinion is significantly changed during the edit and review process!

Always confirm that no comments remain in the document, and all mark-up has been accepted or rejected, before the report is issued.

Readability Statistics

Word also provides a range of tools to evaluate a document's clarity and readability. However, Microsoft's readability statistics can be erratic – Microsoft hasn't quite perfected this part of its software yet. Particularly if the report has a complicated structure, the software can be misled. I don't use readability statistics, but include brief details below for anyone who wishes to experiment. It can be a very imprecise tool, and in my experience the software is "flaky". You may wish to skip over this section.

One criticism of readability statistics is that they focus on sentence length and length of words. You could take a sentence such as this one, and jumble up the words so that it was incomprehensible. The resultant gobbledygook would have the same readability statistics as the comprehensible version.

The following article provides a good summary of some deficiencies in Word's readability checks -

http://www.michbar.org/file/barjournal/article/documents/pdf4article1467.pdf

There are a number of ways to measure verbosity in reports, including average sentence length, percentage of passive sentences, the Flesch-Kincaid grade index, and the Flesch reading ease score. These are included in recent versions of Microsoft Word and, if this option is selected, Word will provide statistics when you run the spell checker.

An example of the readability statistics is shown below.

Readability Statistics	? ✕
Counts	
Words	11812
Characters	60591
Paragraphs	753
Sentences	641
Averages	
Sentences per Paragraph	2.3
Words per Sentence	16.2
Characters per Word	4.9
Readability	
Passive Sentences	17%
Flesch Reading Ease	52.9
Flesch-Kincaid Grade Level	9.8
	OK

Words per Sentence: A useful measure. As noted earlier, average sentence lengths of 15 to 17 words is about right. Become concerned if this is over 20 words. However, if you use bullet points and end each bullet point with a semi-colon or comma, Word 2013 considers the series of bullets to be one sentence until it reaches a period at the end of the bullets. Presenting a number of points in a sentence as bullet points improves readability, but each bullet must end with a period for Word's readability statistics to improve.

Passive sentences: Aim for under 20% of passive sentences.

The following two measures, Flesch Reading Ease and the Flesch-Kincaid Grade Level score a document's readability using formula based on the average sentence length and the average number of syllables per word. They are based on the same measures, but they present their results in slightly different ways. I have made changes that have improved readability according to Flesch Reading Ease, but made readability worse according to Flesch-Kincaid Grade Level. They are only approximate indicators of readability.

Flesch Reading Ease: This test rates text on a 100-point scale. The higher the score, the easier the document is to understand. 90-100 is very easy and 0-29 is very complex and confusing.

For most reports, a score of between 50 and 70 would seem reasonable

The Flesch-Kincaid Grade Level calculates the US school grade level necessary to understand the text. Add five to the grade level to get the minimum age of an average reader to understand the document. For example, grade 9 is 14 to 15 year olds.

To summarise, my experience of running readability statistics in current versions of Word is that they provide erratic results. This part of Word can be very "flaky". I recommend that if used you don't take the Flesch and Flesch-Kincaid Grade Level scores too seriously, and only become concerned if they are extreme.

8. Other Issues

Using British English or American English

If you are working for a global company, you have to decide whether to use British or American English in report writing. The main differences in spelling are:

- The suffix *our* in British English is *or* in American English, e.g. colour, color.
- The suffix *re* in British English is *er* in American English, e.g. metre, meter.
- The suffixes *ize* and *ization* in British English is *ise* and *isation* in American English, e.g. organise, organize.

There are a large number of other minor changes, e.g. double letter l in British English is sometimes single l in American English e.g. *traveller* is *traveler*. The best way to identify these issues is to change the spell checker from U.K. English to American English. This can be done in Word quite simply – see "Language Used Setting" in chapter 7 for more details.

Producing Reports Using PowerPoint

Consultants often report using PowerPoint, and some internal departments are now adopting this format of reporting. Consultants are very sales orientated, and reports are the shop window of their work to senior management. If well written, PowerPoint reports are easy to read, making extensive use of diagrams and charts - a well thought out illustration can be worth a thousand words. Some senior managers prefer PowerPoint reports to wordy narrative reports. There is little benefit in using PowerPoint if the report is simply textual, as a word processing package is more flexible.

However, for the report author, PowerPoint reports can be more difficult to write and update than narrative reports. There is a skill in understanding how to present information effectively in diagrams, graphs and charts, and they are more difficult to create than textual reports. Also, a single report point or section doesn't necessarily fit appropriately onto a single slide. Large consultancy firms that report using PowerPoint often have their own templates, train their staff in using them, and have specialist support functions to edit the presentational elements of reports.

Using PowerPoint to produce reports can also encourage form over substance. If it looks good, there is a tendency to use the visual, even if it adds nothing of substance to the report.

Grading Reports

Many internal audit departments and other review functions provide a grade with reports. This gives the organisation's senior management a simple and unambiguous indicator of the reviewer's opinion of control in the area. From senior management's point of view, it is a real benefit.

However, grading reports can be a contentious issue with the management of the area reviewed. Allocating one simple grade to a report can be subjective and inflammatory, and adversely affect the report author's relationship with management of the area reviewed. This can create difficulties in getting management to agree to the report's findings and recommendations. They may do everything in their power to stall the issue of the report, and react defensively to the findings and recommendations, rather than being open to them.

A compromise is to grade recommendations, the grade representing the reviewer's opinion of the significance of the issue if the recommendation is not implemented. This can be a little less contentious, and some departments feel that as long as recommendations are graded, it is not necessary to grade reports.

If reports are graded, a two-category grading structure is best. The two elements are:

1. The significance of the area. This informs the reader of the importance of the area in the context of the total organisation. This helps the reader assess how much attention to give to the report. The significance can include issues such as financial materiality, legal impact and reputational impact. Letters or numbers (such as

1 or A for very significant, 4 or D for low significance), or words (such as high, medium or low), could be used.

2. The reviewer's evaluation of the state of control in the area. This grade can again be expressed in letters, numbers or words, and/or sometimes colours such as red, amber, green. This summarises in one indicator the reviewer's evaluation, and is the second factor that allows the reader to assess how much attention to give to the report.

Grading reports or just recommendations can provide an opportunity to monitor trends. Statistics such as the number of high, medium and low recommendations made in a period, or the number of reports with unsatisfactory overall gradings can be compiled. This can provide a useful indication of whether control is improving or worsening throughout the organisation.

Improving Report Writing in a Department

Many technical staff are interested in the technical aspects of their role, but see report writing as a chore. Also, if they know that their reports will be reviewed and edited by their managers, they may see little point in going through the laborious task of reviewing and perfecting their own work. So they may present less than perfect work. This is more likely to happen if the assignment is behind schedule, and they are rushing to complete it. But presenting slipshod reports creates more work for their managers, and doesn't help staff members to develop. There are strategies for dealing with this.

1. Document the department reporting style, including the report format, the formality of language and grammar that is expected, and whether British or American English and spelling are to be used.

2. Ensure staff are trained in report writing, and have available suitable reference material such as this guide.

3. Produce a report template for use by authors, or templates if different types of reports are prepared. This will save time in creating reports, enforce a degree of consistency and help to ensure that the layout complies with the department's standards.

4. Emphasise to staff that report writing is a key skill, and that presenting well written reports is a requirement of their current role and for promotion.

5. Ensure staff receive feedback from their management on any reports they draft, and understand why any changes are made.

6. For every assignment, retain a copy of the initial draft report produced by the staff member. As part of the staff member's appraisal, compare this to the final report after it has been edited by management, to assess the quality of their initial draft, and to review any training needs with the staff member.

7. Request feedback from report recipients on the work, including the quality of the report.

Appendix 1

The following list is not exhaustive, but gives examples of longwinded words and phrases, and their alternatives. This will help the reader understand the issue. Some use of words or phrases in the "consider improving" column will not cause a problem in a report, but frequent use of these terms will. The report will become long and turgid, and the key points will be buried in verbiage.

Simplifying Reports by Using Short, Conversational Words

Consider Improving	Good
advantageous	useful
aggregate	total
ascertain	find out
commence	begin or start
completion	end
consequently	so
denote	show
detrimental	harmful
discontinue	stop, end
disseminate	spread
endeavour	try
entitlement	right
erroneous	wrong
fabricate	make
formulate	plan, devise
forthwith	now

Consider Improving	Good
magnitude	size
manufacture	make
methodology	method
notwithstanding	even if
requirement	need
subsequent	later, next
utilisation, utilise, usage	use

Longwinded Expressions to Avoid

a difficult task	difficult
and furthermore	and
as a consequence of	because
as regards to	about
at the moment	now
at the present time	now
attributable to	because of
but nevertheless	nevertheless
by the means of	by
cost the sum of	costs
deemed to be	treated as
despite the fact that	although
due to the fact that	because
during which time	while
expedite the process of	speed up
for the purpose of	for, to
for the reason that	because

Consider Improving	Good
hold in abeyance	wait, postpone
however on the other hand	however
if this was the case	if so
in a clear form	clearly
in a number of cases	don't use. Be specific re numbers, e.g. x out of y tested.
in conjunction with	and, with
in connection with	for, about
in consequence	because
in excess of	more than
in the event that	if
in relation to	about
in respect of	about
in the course of	while, during
in the event	if
in terms of	in
in view of the fact that	as, since, because
is designed to test	tests
may in the future	may, might, could
occasioned by	because of
on numerous occasions	often (but specific numbers far better)
on a daily basis	daily (similar form for weekly, monthly, yearly)
owing to the fact that	as, since, because
previous to	before
provided that	if
so as to ensure that	to ensure
subsequent to	after
take action to	(usually unnecessary, omit)
that being the case	if
the fact of the matter is	the fact is (or omit entirely)

Consider Improving	Good
the month of	(omit)
time period	(use one word, not both)
under the provisions of	under
until such time that	until
was in need of	needed

Redundant Words, Including Intensifiers

absolute certainty	certainty
advanced notice	notice
advanced planning	planning
advanced warning	warning
clearly	(consider omitting)
consensus of opinion	consensus
difficult challenge	challenge
end result	result
future prospects	prospects
general consensus	consensus
joint agreement	agreement
key	(consider omitting)
past experience	experience
part history	history
reasonable	(consider omitting)
remove completely	remove
significant	(consider omitting)
special	(consider omitting)
successfully complete	complete
very	(consider omitting)

Using Verbs Rather than Nouns

Consider Improving	Good
give consideration to	consider
the audit team conducted an investigation of	the audit team investigated
the auditor has no expectation that	the auditor does not expect that
the avoidance of	avoid
the clarification of	clarify
the delivery of	deliver
the development of	develop
the discussion concerned x	x was discussed
the improvement of	improve

Appendix 2

Some Commonly Confused Words

Many English words can be confused. In several decades of editing reports, the following are examples of the more common words I have found to be confused. The use of the alternative word would not be picked up by a spell checker.

Advice/Advise
In British English advice is the noun, **advise** is the verb. In American English **advise** will be used for both the verb and the noun.

Adverse/Averse
Adverse means difficult or opposing, such as adverse trading conditions. **Averse** means you don't like it, as in "averse to rules".

Affect/Effect
Usually **affect** is a verb, and **effect** a noun. As in to **affect** a change. The **effect** is the result of the change. However, increasingly authors are not making a distinction.

Compliment/Complement
Compliment means to praise. **Complement** means to accompany, or to supplement. An alternative mean of **complement** is quota or amount. Both words can be verbs or nouns.

Criterion/Criteria
Criterion is the singular, **criteria** the plural.

Discreet/Discrete
Discreet means subtle or unassuming. **Discrete** means unconnected.

Disinterested /Uninterested
Disinterested means unbiased. **Uninterested** means indifferent, not caring about.

Principal/Principle

Principal means the main or the chief. It can also mean head teacher. **Principle** means belief or ethical value, or a basic rule. "In **principle**" is a special use of the word, which means that someone agrees with a concept, but may have concerns about the practical application.

Program/Programme

In British English **program** means a computer program, whereas **programme** means an itinerary, or a television or radio show. In American English, **program** has both meanings.

Simple/Simplistic

Simple means easy or straightforward. **Simplistic** means naïve, foolishly simple.

Stationary/Stationery

Stationary means not moving. Remember by the a in parking. **Stationery** is paper, pens etc. Remember by the e in envelopes.

Appendix 3

Suggested Answers

3a) Complaints Case Study – Identifying Unnecessary Words and Phrases

The draft on page 21 contains many "dead wood" words and phrases, which could be omitted or reworded. The worst examples appear below.

Bad	Better
the development of this spreadsheet	the spreadsheet was
is used to perform an analysis of	analyses
on a weekly basis	weekly
in order	omit
and produces a presentation of	presents
the end result of this is a spreadsheet	the spreadsheet
with regards to the spreadsheet logic, this	the spreadsheet logic
subject to a review	reviewed
in view of the fact that	as
another weakness is that	omit
a very difficult task	difficult
in relation to	of
because of this, we consider	we consider
end result would be	result in
in addition	omit
because if the above weaknesses	omit
it is our recommendation	we recommend
carry out a review of	review
after this review has taken place	omit
usual	omit

Where text has been deleted rather than changed, a line has been put through the text in the before section.

In the "after" text below, changes have been presented in bold.

BEFORE TEXT	AFTER THE DEAD WOOD HAS BEEN REMOVED
Complaints statistics are prepared for the Customer Services Review Committee and the Board by manually inputting data from the complaints management system into an Excel spreadsheet. The development of this spreadsheet took place in the Customer Services department, and it is used to perform an analysis of complaints data on a weekly basis in various ways ~~in order~~ to show trends and changes, and produces a presentation of the output using a series of charts. Although the complaints management system provides the raw data, this system does not have sophisticated analysis and visual presentation tools.	Complaints statistics are prepared for the Customer Services Review Committee and the Board by manually inputting data from the complaints management system into an Excel spreadsheet. **The spreadsheet was developed** in the Customer Services department, and it **analyses** complaints data **weekly** in various ways to show trends and changes, and **presents** the output using a series of charts. Although the complaints management system provides the raw data, this system does not have sophisticated analysis and visual presentation tools.
The spreadsheet was prepared by Mr A Smith, a Complaints Handling Officer, and a computer enthusiast without a formal I.T. background. The end result of this is a spreadsheet with major weaknesses as outlined below.	The spreadsheet was prepared by Mr A Smith, a Complaints Handling Officer, and a computer enthusiast without a formal I.T. background. **The spreadsheet** has major weaknesses as outlined below.
~~With regards to~~ the spreadsheet logic, ~~this~~ has not been subject to a review and there is not a formal testing process in place when	The spreadsheet logic has not been **reviewed** and there is not a formal testing process in place when developing the formula. The system is still being

developing the formula. The system is still being enhanced and changes are made regularly. However, in view of the fact that there is no version control system in place, there is a risk that a wrong version of a spreadsheet could be used. We are also concerned that neither the code nor the data is backed up, or subject to the organisation's contingency arrangements. ~~Another weakness is that~~ the spreadsheet logic is undocumented, making maintenance by anyone other than Mr Smith a very difficult task.

Data is input manually from the complaints handling system, without a formal checking process. Therefore, there is a risk in relation to input errors being undetected.

Because of this, we consider this is a very high significance issue as errors could result in complaints trends going undetected. This would delay corrective action, and the end result would be poor customer service. ~~In addition,~~ this could also result in regulatory breaches.

Recommendations

~~Because of the above weaknesses~~ it is our recommendation that the spreadsheet be placed under the control of the I.T. department, which should carry out a review

enhanced and changes are made regularly. However, as there is no version control system in place, there is a risk that a wrong version of a spreadsheet could be used. We are also concerned that neither the code nor the data is backed up, or subject to the organisation's contingency arrangements. The spreadsheet logic is undocumented, making maintenance by anyone other than Mr Smith difficult.

Data is input manually from the complaints handling system, without a formal checking process. Therefore there is a risk of input errors being undetected. We consider this is a very high significance issue as errors could result in complaints trends going undetected. This would delay corrective action, and result in poor customer service. This could also result in regulatory breaches.

Recommendations

We recommend that the spreadsheet be placed under the control of the I.T. department, which should review the logic, and then place the system under

of the logic, and then ~~after this review has taken place,~~ place the system under the ~~usual~~ controls for a production system. Furthermore, the Customer Services Department should introduce a checking process for data manually input to the system, to identify any data input errors. (Significance Very High).	the controls for a production system. Furthermore, the Customer Services Department should introduce a checking process for data manually input to the system, to identify any data input errors. (Significance Very High).

3b) Complaints Case Study - Changes for Structure and Tone

Identifying "dead wood" words and phrases is only part of the editing process. In the reworked example below, further changes have been made:

1. We start at the end and provide an overview of the conclusion before providing the evidence. This orientates the reader, and helps them understand the issues more quickly.
2. We give some credit to the department for their initiative in developing the spreadsheet. This seems fair, and is likely to result in a more positive and constructive response from the department.
3. We use lists in two places, rather than dense text. Readers generally find it easier to understand lists or bullet points, rather than lengthy, rambling text.

Complaints Reporting Example

Weaknesses in Locally Developed Complaints Management System. Significance: Very High

We identified integrity concerns with the Excel spreadsheet used to analyse complaint data for senior management and the Board.

The complaints management system is used to process complaints from the receipt of the complaint to its conclusion. However, this system does not have sophisticated analysis and management information facilities. Therefore the Customer Services Department developed a spreadsheet to analyse complaints data.

The system developed is a sophisticated Excel spreadsheet. Data is manually input in summary form from the complaints management system into the spreadsheet. It is then analysed in various ways to show trends in complaint type, changes in complaint volume over time, and numbers of complaints addressed within different periods. This analysis is displayed on a series of charts. The output from the spreadsheet is used by management in the department, the Customer Services Review Committee and the Board.

The spreadsheet was developed by a Complaints Handling Officer who is a computer enthusiast, but without a formal I.T. background. We applaud his initiative, and the Customer Services Department for recognising the need for easy-to-understand visual reporting. However a project of this importance and complexity should have been referred to the I.T. department.

The spreadsheet system has the following weaknesses:

1. The logic has not been reviewed and there is not a formal testing process in place when developing the formula.

2. The system is still being enhanced. However, there is no version control system, and therefore a wrong version of a spreadsheet could be used.

3. Neither the code or the data is backed up, or subject to contingency arrangements

4. The spreadsheet logic is undocumented. Therefore maintenance by anyone other than the developer would be difficult.

5. Data is input manually from the complaints handling system, without any checking. Therefore there is a risk of input errors being undetected.

Errors could result in complaints trends going undetected. This would delay corrective action, and result in poor customer service. In addition, this could result in regulatory breaches.

Recommendations

We recommend that:

1. The spreadsheet is placed under the control of the I.T. department, which should review the logic, and then place the system under the usual controls for a production system. (Significance: Very High).
2. The Customer Services Department introduces a checking process for data manually input to the system, to identify any data input errors. (Significance: Very High).

3c) Proofreading Exercise

Proofreading Exercise from Chapter 6, Page 30

Original text, error free according to Word 2013:

> There are a number of mistakes in this paragraph. Some of them would not be detected buy an automated spell and crammer chick. How many thongs can you find wrong. It is no easy, particularly if you have too reed a long, badly structured piper, with manly moor tissues.

Text with amendments:

> There are a number of mistakes in this paragraph. Some of them would not be detected ~~buy~~ by an automated spell and ~~crammer~~ grammar ~~chick~~ check. How many ~~thongs~~ things can you find wrong? It is ~~no~~ not easy, particularly if you have ~~too reed~~ to read a long, badly structured ~~piper~~ paper, with ~~manly~~ many ~~moor~~ more ~~tissues~~ issues.

It is fairly easy to identify these errors – it is only one paragraph and the reader is concentrating on finding typographical errors. However, it is much easier to miss a small number of errors in many pages to text, and particularly if you are reviewing the structure and meaning of the text as well. That is why it is important to do a final read-through just looking for typographical errors.

Dear Reader

This book is intended as a concise, inexpensive guide to writing reports that will result in management action. If you have found it useful, I would be very grateful if you would review it on the retailer's website. I am an independent author and so, unlike a major publisher, I don't have a marketing department. Therefore I depend on satisfied readers to help publicise the book.

Kind regards

Ian Douglas

Printed in Poland
by Amazon Fulfillment
Poland Sp. z o.o., Wrocław